Contents

Rear Tenement Bedroom, Lower East Side, New York City, c.1910.

1: Immigrants and Literature

He is an American, who, leaving behind him all his ancient prejudices and manners, receives new ones from the mode of life he has embraced, the new government he obeys, and the new rank he holds. He becomes an American by being received in the broad lap of our great *Alma Mater*. Here individuals of all nations are melted into a new race of men, whose labours and posterity will one day cause great changes in the world.

Hector St. John de Crèvecoeur, 1782[1]

The immigrant experience constitutes a central shaping force of American culture. Many of the myths which form an inherent part of the idea of America originate in the dreams and experiences of the millions who migrated from the Old to the New World. These have been related and analysed not only by historians but also by literary artists, who have presented a more subjective, more humanized, sometimes more didactic, depiction of the immigrant past. As Henry Seidel Canby has written,

Literature can be used, and has been magnificently used by Americans, in the service of history, of science, of religion, or of political propaganda. It has no sharp boundaries, though it passes through broad margins from art into instruction or argument. The writing or speech of a culture such as ours which has been so closely bound to the needs of a rapidly growing, democratic nation, moves quickly into the utilitarian, . . . in a literature which is most revealing when studied as a by product of American experience.[2]

In much literature written by Europeans as well as in that of their American descendants, there is a wealth of writing about the immigrant experience. It is not always the product of direct observation, quite often being written by those who stayed behind or by the descendants of the actual immigrants. Different national groups have been associated with different periods of immigration and specific themes. In British literature it mostly takes the form of writing about the problems of settlement and colonization. In French writing it is more often associated with a romantic dream of freedom as in the agrarian optimism of Crèvecoeur or the sentimentalization of the noble savage in Chateaubriand.

In the nineteenth century the experience itself was broadened as it became associated with the migrations of different classes and national types: Germans, Irish, Italians, East and Middle Europeans and Scandinavians, to name the most important groups. The phenomenon also assumed massive proportions, with thirty-five million immigrants arriving in the United States between 1800 and 1924 — the largest voluntary migration of people in history. The literature produced by this wave of immigration — whether autobiographical or fictional, whether written by participants or their descendants or by those whose imagination was fired by contact with immigrants — tends to concentrate rather on the problems of adjustment to a new environment and assimilation into a society that had already established a definite white 'Anglo-Saxon' and Protestant (or WASP) character.

There have been two distinctive traditions in this last stream of immigrant writing, each of them focussing on one of the two essential destinations of the immigrant — the land or the city. It is of course no accident that the Scandinavians were primarily responsible for developing the literature about immigrant settlement on the land, especially in the West, nor that Jewish immigrant writers took for their preserve the American city with its promise of freedom and problems of assimilation and secularization. The contribution of these two literatures to American thought and culture is incalculable, and it is with them and associated works that this essay will primarily concern itself.

2: The Frontier and Scandinavian Pioneers

The West and the frontier, by the mid-nineteenth century, had come to occupy a central place in the American imagination. Just as generations of Europeans had long believed that a land of opportunity lay across the Atlantic, so Americans saw great opportunities beckoning them to cross the Appalachians into the great Mississippi valley. Not merely was the West the route to fabled wealth, but this fertile heartland could be transformed into an agrarian paradise, a new Garden of Eden tilled by yeoman farmers, economically self-sufficient and spiritually enriched by their closeness to Nature. This Jeffersonian attitude found its expression in literature, in James Fenimore Cooper's Leatherstocking, the epitome of the "natural gentleman," and in Walt Whitman's aspirations for a thrusting, democratic people. These optimistic views of frontier life were expressed, however, at a time when most pioneers were American-born and the area being settled lay primarily east of the Mississippi. Not until after the civil war did immigrants, mainly from Northern Europe, contribute significantly to westward expansion, on the prairies and plains west of the great river. The imaginative writers marked by this immigrant experience significantly changed the way the conquest of the wilderness gained expression in works of literature.

Scandinavians, in particular, played a major role in the settlement of the Far West. Neither Norway nor Sweden could support its population because of the nature of its laws of inheritance and a dearth of productive soil. "Between 1825 and 1914 . . . Norway lost a higher proportion of her people through emigration to America than any other European country except Ireland."[3] In Sweden, the 1860s saw both an economic crisis and three years of crop failures which came to be known as "The Great Famine" (1865-68). Thousands of Swedes left for the New World at this time, attracted by the cheap or free land provided by the Homestead Act of 1862, or offered by the railroad companies to intending settlers.

Rölvaag and Moberg

Although many novels were written during the nineteenth century by Scandinavian-American authors, especially Norwegians, very few have been translated and the literary value of those that has is not high. It is largely in the twentieth century that fiction of literary distinction describing Scandinavian-American settlement in America has been created. Most notably, Ole Edvart Rölvaag and Vilhelm Moberg both wrote trilogies describing the experiences of their forbears in America — Rölvaag for the Norwegians, Moberg for the Swedes. In both trilogies, it is the first novels — *Giants in The Earth* (1927) and *The Emigrants* (1951) — which are most successful as literature and deserve most attention. Both authors wrote about immigrant pioneers, and stressed the frustrations of the journey from Europe or across America or both, the difficulties of actually settling on the frontier, the importance of the family for survival, and the conflict which developed between the first and second generations. The issue of assimilation into American society was also an important concern to Rölvaag and to some other Scandinavian authors.

Though concerned with the fate of individual characters, Rölvaag and Moberg both stress the importance of the survival and success of the group in forming outposts of the Old World in the New and eventually relinquishing Europe to embrace America. *Giants in The Earth* opens with Per Hansa and his party already pushing across the American prairie toward their new home; *The Emigrants* begins in the Old World and ends with the Swedish emigrants setting foot on

American soil for the first time. Sophus Winther comments:

It is of value to note that the emigrant novel has a longer history than the picaresque story, that it is more profoundly rooted in human experience, and it concerns itself with the struggle of man for the primary needs of existence, ... with a representative group, sometimes a whole people. But whether the characters are few or many, their adventures grow out of a desire to escape from bondage into a new world where the spirit of man may achieve the freedoms necessary to a full life.[4]

This struggle is vividly depicted throughout both Rölvaag's and Moberg's trilogies in what is basically a realistic form: the meticulous presentation of characters, environment and their interrelation.

Giants in the Earth and The Emigrants successfully evoke the pioneer experience because of their authors' powers of description and characterization. Rölvaag's evocation of the prairie presents both its startling beauty and its horrific aspects. Eschewing understatement, he presents a winter evening in highly metaphorical and visually imagistic phrases:

... Evenings ... magic, still evenings, surpassing in beauty the most fantastic dreams of childhood! ... Out to the westward — so surprisingly near — a blazing countenance sank to the rest on a white couch ... set it afire ... kindled a radiance ... a golden flame that flowed in many streams from horizon to horizon ....

The numerous ellipses slow one's reading of the passage and give a sense of things unsaid, of the ineffable quality of the experience described. Set against this description is one of a far different sort: "Monsterlike the Plain lay there — sucked in her breath one week, and the next week blew it out again. Man she scorned; his works she would not brook .... She would know, when the time came, how to guard herself and her own against him!" This sentience of the prairie pervades the novel to such an extent that the setting becomes an active element in the depiction of the characters, who must pit themselves against it.[5]

Moberg's descriptive powers in The Emigrants are seen most clearly in his documentary depiction of conditions in Sweden for poor farmers. In preparing to leave for America, we are told that "Kristina packed eight rye-meal loaves and twenty of barley, a wooden tub of strongly salted butter, two quarts of honey, one cheese, half a dozen smoked sausages, a quarter of smoked lamb, a piece of salt pork, and some twenty salted herrings." But alongside this matter-of-fact listing of items, one also finds a highly sensuous prose:

The fire sparkled and all enjoyed the coziness of the inn after the cold road. Their senses as well as their limbs thawed. There was an odor of food and brännvin, snuff and chewing tobacco, greased leather and warm, wet wadmal [coarse woollen clothing], there was a fragrance of mothers' milk as the women suckled the children.

The details are preserved, but are evocatively presented as they impinge on the consciousness of the characters. This creative use of

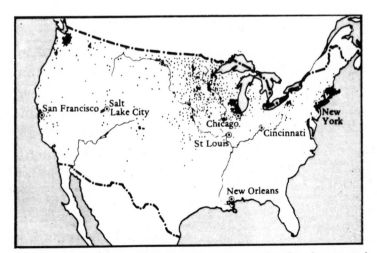

This map shows the location of the two-and-a-quarter million Scandinavians who had settled in the United States by 1920. Many lived in metropolitan areas, especially on the East Coast and near Chicago, but Scandinavians, along with the Germans, were distinctive among immigrant groups in that so many of them chose to settle in frontier areas, especially in Minnesota, Iowa, Wisconsin and the Dakotas.

detail is more characteristic of Rölvaag's style than the mere piling up of facts which Moberg frequently resorts to.[6]

Rölvaag presents American nature as inimical to man, and the characterization reflects the settlers' abilities to respond to the challenges of this hostile environment. Thus, Beret mirrors Old World attitudes in her fatalistic and superstitious fear of this new environment; whereas, as Joseph Baker puts it, "her husband, Per Hansa, is a man of the West; he glories in the fact that he is an American free-willer, self-asserting. He rebels against destiny and tries to master nature." Baker even sees the struggle presented in cosmic terms: "Here the pioneer struggle with the untamed universe may serve as a symbol for the condition of man himself against inhuman destiny."[7]

The characterization in *The Emigrants* elicited some hostile criticism from Swedish critics on account of the dialogue of the peasants. The earthy language which they employed, particularly that of Ulrika, the parish whore, and Jonas Petter, who enjoys telling vulgar stories, scandalized some readers, despite Moberg's insistence that this was the way they actually spoke. Indeed, it is the characterization which primarily accounts for the novel's realism. Moberg manages to combine a great deal of factual information with a warmth of characterization, and by making empathy with the characters possible, the facts are humanized and dramatized.

One must be careful in appraising the *literal* truthfulness of the factual information presented in *The Emigrants*. All of Moberg's aunts and uncles had gone to America, and there were many letters and photographs from them to which he had access. He relied upon answers to direct questions which he posed in letters to individuals who had been involved in the migration and upon historical documents. Thus, the information was decidedly of second-hand origin. He did finally decide to emigrate in 1948, having almost done so over thirty years earlier. Indeed, part of *The Emigrants* was written in Sweden and part in America, the remaining volumes of what in Swedish was a tetralogy being written in the United States. Philip Holmes points out that

> The documentary elements of the novel are partly based on historical evidence, and are partly Moberg's own creation. So much is real that the remainder, the merely realistic, takes on the illusion of reality. For example Gunnar Eidevall made the surprising discovery that the population figures given in the novel for Ljuder on 1 January 1846 have no basis in reality.[8]

The essential truth of the novel, however, lies in Moberg's depiction of the combination of historical and cultural forces which drove the emigrants from their homeland (poverty, a rigid class structure, religious persecution) and the emotional effects of these forces and of the uprooting to which they led. One critic has noted that "Moberg does not always succeed in subordinating his data to the lives of his people. At times he writes a sort of romantic history."[9] At other times Moberg drifts into the style of a history where documentation takes over from the characters rather than providing support for them. This is why *The Emigrants* is ultimately not as successful artistically as Rölvaag's earlier *Giants in the Earth,* where the characters are always kept in focus and the facts of their experiences are seen in terms of and never detached from their own inner lives.

The strugggle for survival is dramatized in *Giants in the Earth* through a series of concretely realised events which stress rising action leading to dramatic tension. One instance of this occurs when Per Hansa appears to have planted his wheat too early and firmly believes that the frost has killed it all. When the first green shoots appear above the earth, Per Hansa's boundless relief and thanksgiving is vividly dramatized:

> There he stood spellbound, gazing at the sight spread before him. His whole body shook; tears came to his eyes, so that he found it difficult to see clearly. And well he might be surprised. Over the whole field tiny shoots were quivering in the warm sunshine.
>
> Store-Hans was standing now by his father's side; he looked at him in consternation.
>
> "Are you sick, father?"
>
> No answer.
>
> "Why you're crying!"
>
> "You're . . . so — foolish, Store-Hans!"[10]

Rölvaag wrote this novel at a time when a shift was taking place in American literary styles. At the end of the nineteenth and beginning of the twentieth centuries Naturalism, with its stress upon determinism and concern with the excesses of an industrial civilization, tended to avoid a close scrutiny of characters as individuals and concerned itself rather with the impersonal forces that shaped them. By the time *Giants in the Earth* was being written (1923-24), a change had already occurred in the literary approach to character, "a shift from the sociological to the psychological. It is no longer the world of objective fact that obtrudes as the significant reality, but the subtler world of emotional experience." While one is constantly aware of the prairie as a force, the focus of attention is directed more upon the moods and emotions of the characters. It is through this depiction of the emotional reactions to the pioneer experience that Rölvaag transcends mere documentary. As V.L Parrington has written,

> With the growth of a maturer realism we are beginning to understand how great was the price exacted by the frontier; and it is because *Giants in the Earth*, for the first time in our fiction, evaluates adequately the settlement in terms of emotion, because it penetrates to the secret inner life of men and women who undertook the heavy work of subduing the wilderness, that it is — quite apart from all artistic values — a great historical document.[11]

Rölvaag wrote all three novels of the trilogy in Norwegian, in America. He was not a pioneer himself, having arrived in the United States in 1896 and worked on his uncle's farm in South Dakota for three years. However, he did possess a knowledge of the psychology of ordinary Norwegian farmers. He understood, also, what it meant to be an immigrant — artistic imagination could provide the rest. Thus, despite the fact that *Giants in the Earth* is set in the 1870s and early 80s, almost twenty years before Rölvaag set foot on American soil, Julius Olson's comment is still valid: "For a novel of our pioneers may, if well done, present the history of our pioneers in a nutshell. It will be history which never happened quite as it is presented, but which is essentially true nevertheless."[12]

Neither Rölvaag nor Moberg succeeded in producing novels of equal literary quality to *Giants in the Earth* or *The Emigrants* in the later works of their respective trilogies. In *Peder Victorious* (1929) and *Their Father's God* (1931), where Rölvaag is concerned with the generational, cultural, religious, and social issues confronting an established community, the quality of description, characterization, and dramatic tension is not as impressive as that in *Giants in the Earth*. In *Peder Victorious*, Beret's desire to preserve her son's "Norwegianness" founders as Peder becomes more and more American in speech and customs. This pseudo-sociological approach incorporating inadequately fictionalized materials continues in *Their Father's God* where the conflicts are religious and social, with the negative results of assimilation being stressed. One of Rölvaag's basic beliefs was that a strong ethnic culture made for a strong and stable America, and he worked all his life to preserve Norwegian culture in America.

Moberg is not so concerned with issues of assimilation. In *Unto a Good Land* (1954) and *The Last Letter Home* (1961), the main themes revolve about the problems of arriving at the place of settlement, the settlement itself, and the growth of prosperity. Half of *Unto a Good Land* is concerned with inland travel in America, presented through a great deal of detail; the other half describes the place and process of settlement. The continent itself provides the unifying factor: its vastness and the effect of this upon the consciousness of the travellers contrasts with a focus upon one spot. *The Last Letter Home* traces the story of the settlers for almost forty years, ending in 1890 with the death of the protagonist, Karl Oskar, who expresses satisfaction in his emigration. Although both novels contain individual scenes which possess a high degree of dramatic tension, neither is as satisfying as *The Emigrants*.

In this trilogy, when Moberg's style works well, as it often does, the sharpness of characterization is not blurred by the documentation which fills all three works. The main characters are presented vividly in thought, action and language, Moberg's commitment to an overall realistic approach remaining strong throughout. The trilogy stands as a major statement of the Swedish immigrant experience in America, and along with Rölvaag's treatment of Norwegian settlers, graphically depicts the opening and settlement of the American frontier by these two important groups.

Lesser Lights — and Willa Cather

The issue of assimilation is one which occupied a number of Scandinavian writers besides Rölvaag. Hjalmar Hjorth Boyesen and Hans Mattson both believed, unlike Rölvaag, that the best course for their respective peoples was complete assimilation into American society. Boyesen was Norwegian and had emigrated to the United States in 1869. His novel *Falconberg* (1878) is set almost entirely in America and is concerned with immigrants in the Norwegian settlement at Pine Ridge, Wisconsin (called "Hardanger" in the novel). Through the protagonist, Einer Falconberg, Boyesen states his attitude toward Americanization:

> Here in this wondrous land a new and great people is being born; a new and great civilization, superior to any the world has ever seen, is in the process of formation. It would be a foolish and ineffectual labor if we were to cling to our inherited language and traditional prejudices, and endeavor to remain a small isolated tribe.[13]

The similarity to Crèvecoeur's viewpoint, expressed in the epigraph on page 5, is clear: Americanization demands the giving up of Old

Country traditions for the benefits of being completely involved in the creation of a new society. That this 'melting' process did not take place as thoroughly as Crèvecoeur thought it would or as Boyesen desired does not lessen the forcefulness of their sense of the nature of the American experiment: the belief that the American was a man with new principles and ideas who would have a profound effect upon the rest of the world.

This exhortation to assimilate can also be seen in Hans Mattson's autobiography, *Reminiscences: The Story of an Emigrant*, published in English in 1892. Mattson traces his life from his childhood in Sweden through a spectacularly successful career in America, where he became not only a Union colonel in the Civil War but Consul General of the United States in India. He states at the outset that he "owes whatever he has accomplished in life to the opportunities offered by the free institutions of this country." While full of praise for America, he retains some affection for his birthplace, "its people and institutions." But the attitude of the Swedish aristocracy toward the common people and work appals him, and he feels that it is the respect for what an individual can do, rather than for his background, that makes America great. Citing experiences from his travels in many countries, he concludes that "the only desirable immigrants to this country are those who cease to be foreigners, and merge right into the American nation."[14]

The style of the two works is very different. Boyesen's is stilted and literary, tricked out with allusions and references in Latin, Greek, and Italian which seem out of place in the wilderness of "Hardanger." By describing events in his life in simple, non-figurative prose, Mattson, on the other hand, creates a heightened sense of reality. In spite of the selection of incidents which any autobiographer makes, Mattson's account illustrates how historical events can be personalized and humanized through autobiography.

Like Mattson, Boyesen was an immigrant. He lived in and studied Norwegian communities in the Midwest, and through many stories, poems and the novel *Falconberg* attempted to present "the Scandinavian to the American reader by a discussion of the scenery, traditions, and characteristics of Scandinavia. Secondly, he discussed what immigration meant, to both the new and the old country, and to the individual Scandinavian himself." Despite its stylistic weaknesses, *Falconberg* does illustrate some of the problems faced by Norwegian pioneers. Boyesen was "The first Norwegian to use English successfully as a literary language, and to find a place in American literature."[15] Both he and Mattson, like Rölvaag and Moberg, depict in their writing the struggles, both physical and emotional, of Scandinavian pioneers trying to come to grips with the New World.

Willa Cather's insights into the physical and psychological problems faced by pioneers and their offspring, and her ability to create effective novels from these insights, justify her inclusion here despite the fact that she was neither a pioneer nor an immigrant. In *O Pioneers!* (1913), *The Song of the Lark* (1915) and *My Ántonia* (1918) can be seen the influence of a decade spent in a rural community in Nebraska, which had been settled primarily by Norwegians and Bohemians. When she arrived in Nebraska in 1883, at the age of ten, her family was surprised to discover that "native-born Americans were in the minority on the divide . . . . During the 1870s Nebraska grew by 310 percent, and it was no accident that foreign settlement comprised the majority of this growth. In fact, twenty-three nations were represented among the purchasers of Burlington land."[16] Her first novel concerned with pioneers (the second novel she wrote) contains references to Swedes, Norwegians, Germans, Russians, Bohemians, and Frenchmen.

O Pioneers! (the title borrowed from Walt Whitman's paean to the settlers of the American frontier) and *The Song of the Lark* both concern courageous women, but stress very different aspects of the frontier experience. In *O Pioneers!* Alexandra Bergson dreams of the world beyond the farm but is devoted to the land, which provides the major unifying factor in the novel. Cather presents her "as a kind of Earth Mother or Corn Goddess, a Ceres who presides over the fruitful land, symbol of the success of the pioneers in taming the reluctant but immensely promising soil."[17] She has the centrality of place of Per Hansa or Karl Oskar, both of whom are forward-looking and, along with a most necessary sense of practicality, can view the land in a non-materialistic and spiritual sense.

By contrast, Thea Kronborg, in *The Song of the Lark*, like Alexandra a second-generation Swedish-American, is most concerned with leaving the small Colorado town where she was raised, to achieve artistic success in the wider world as a singer. In the preface Cather states that she had originally intended to call the novel *Artist's Youth*, to "tell of an artist's awakening and struggle; her floundering escape from a smug, domestic, self-satisfied provincial world of utter ignorance."[18] This attitude parallels that expressed in Sinclair Lewis' novel *Main Street* (1920), where the Midwest has become a place of limited vision, materialism, and conventional morality. Rölvaag's and Moberg's heroic male pioneers have no place in *The Song of the Lark* and *Main Street;* in *O Pioneers!*, however, Cather shows how this heroism can be carried on by a woman.

In *My Ántonia* (1918) Cather presents the quintessential pioneer woman. Ántonia Shimerda was born in Bohemia and arrived in Nebraska as a young girl. She develops the ability to overcome

Life on the Great Plains was lonely and hard, with living conditions made particularly difficult by the lack of timber. This photograph, taken by J. N. Templeton in 1885, shows a pioneer family's sod-house in the Dakotas.

hardships and retain her sense of life's worth. Not only does she represent the prairie country to Cather and Jim Burden, the narrator, but "She lent herself to immemorial human attitudes which we recognize by instinct as universal and true . . . . She was a rich mine of life, like the founders of early races."[19] Like Alexandra Bergson and Thea Kronborg, Ántonia must overcome many difficulties. The main difference between her and the previous two heroines is that while they are working toward a specific career goal — Alexandra, the prosperity of her farm; Thea, artistic achievement — Ántonia is concerned just with living fully.

H.L. Mencken claimed to "know of no novel that makes the remote folk of the western prairies more real than *My Ántonia* makes them, and I know of none that makes them seem better worth knowing." And Granville Hicks pays a similar tribute to her blend of observation and imaginative skill when he reminds us that, "After all, Miss Cather saw at first hand the Nebraska of the eighties and nineties, and her accounts of the life there are not without authenticity. However much she emphasizes the heroism and piety of the pioneers, she does not neglect the hardships and sacrifices."[20]

An important difference between *My Ántonia* and the other two novels lies in the choice of a different point of view. Cather tells the story through the eyes of Jim Burden, thus distancing herself from the material. We see Ántonia in terms of what she means to Jim: as someone with whom he grew up and who, after he has left her for a larger world, remains imprinted on his memory. For the reader, Jim Burden's life in the larger world only serves to heighten the admiration felt for the one who stayed at home, for Ántonia's struggle for a place in life and her ultimate discovery of the right niche for her — rearing a large family on a prairie farm.

Stylistically, *My Ántonia* marks an improvement over *The Song of the Lark* in that Cather does not indulge in the large-scale use of unimpressive detail which she used to depict the various stages of Thea Kronborg's career in the earlier novel. Similarly, *My Ántonia* exhibits a greater literary skill than *O Pioneers!* in which "there is much description and elucidation of character; in *My Ántonia* comparatively little, the people being so solidly set before us that little is needed."[21] All three novels contain, however, strong characterizations, and all three present heroines who symbolize the drive and determination of the best of the pioneers. Similarly, all three novels condemn the materialism of those individuals who have lost the ability to dream and who desire only a sterile conformity which Cather sees as greatly at odds with the spirit which brought the first generation from the Old to the New World.

Although there were great differences in the experiences of the pioneers on the frontier and those of immigrants in cities, there were important similarities as well. Immigrants who settled in both environments had been uprooted from the Old World and were determined to succeed in the New; something which many in both areas failed to do. As we shall see, the struggle for survival in the cities as presented in autobiography and fiction may have lacked some of the romance of the struggle of the pioneers on the frontier; however, dreams existed in both environments, as did courage and the fortitude necessary to overcome often hostile surroundings. City immigrants had a 'frontier' of their own with which to contend.

3: The City and the Jewish Tradition

Mass immigration to the American city coincided with — and largely contributed to — a massive growth in the size of cities. Immigrants settled in the great cities because of the many opportunites they offered, not least the multitude of unskilled jobs provided by the industrial revolution of the age. However, the rapid growth of the city brought with it many difficulties: economic life became more structured and impersonal, and social divisions widened as rich and poor came to inhabit different districts of the city. The uncertainties of the new industrial order were compounded by the worst consequences of rapid urban growth — low wages, appalling housing conditions, bad sanitation, and high levels of morbidity and mortality amid the squalor — and the immigrants, themselves coming mainly from peasant communities, suffered the hardship, degradation and disillusionment undergone by many migrants, American and foreign, who moved into industrial metropolises. In the city, the immigrant experience was complicated by involvement in the fundamental social and economic changes that were transforming America in the late nineteenth and early twentieth centuries.

Irish, Italians and Jews

This experience was shared by many different ethnic groups, and many of them have left some record of it in literature. The Irish were the first to establish themselves strongly in the burgeoning cities, but have not produced a major author to chronicle their experiences. The most skilful Irish-American author to come close is James T. Farrell in his *Studs Lonigan* trilogy (1932-35), which focuses on second and third-generation immigrants. This impressive naturalistic series, filled with detailed social observation, traces the decline and finally, the destruction of a young man who, in spite of his parents' early hopes, gives in to the wrong influences in his urban environment and becomes a brutal barbarian. Some immigrants, like Studs' house-painter father, do improve themselves socially and economically, but it is too easy for lower-class Irish children in Chicago to adopt twisted versions of the American dream — which, in Studs' case, finally destroys him.[22]

Like the Irish, the Italians came to the United States in large numbers (over four million in both cases), settled mainly in the great cities, and produced impressive, if minor, novelists interested in the immigrant experience. For example, Guido D'Agostino, born in New York City in 1906, was particularly concerned with the problems of cultural assimilation. In *Olives On The Apple Tree* (1940), he contrasts Emile, a doctor who wishes to gain acceptance in upper-middle-class society, and Marco, a failure who cannot accept the harsh competitiveness of America. Marco sees Americans as never satisfied, and himself prefers the old Italian warmth and sense of community, "the conversation, the laughing and everything else that makes life worthwhile." Italians who try to leave their old culture in a headlong rush to become American not only deprive American society of something valuable but cheat themselves:

> No more the Italian but a bastard Italian. Quick he forgets everything from the old country to make money and have a car and buy food in cans and become just like the American he is working for. But he does not become the American and he is no more the Italian. Something in the middle — no good for himself and no good for the country. A real bastardo.

Even Emile eventually achieves real peace of mind only when he returns to live with other Italian-Americans.[23]

The best known Italian-American novel is undoubtedly *The Godfather* (1969), written by Mario Puzo, who was born in New York City in 1920. However, his skilful and dramatic novel, *The Fortunate Pilgrim* (1964), is more revealing, for it deals with the problems of a first-generation immigrant family in the 1930s. The family is held together by a powerful, domineering mother, Lucia Santa, a matriarch determined to set her children on the road to a successful life in the United States. Around them are irresistible pressures towards Americanization, and a society that rewards unethical practices; as Lucia Santa says of one local Italian family who are successful criminals, "What animals. And yet when they have money they dare look everyone in the eye." Many characters are culturally adrift, and the combination of new values and the depression becomes too much for them. Lucia Santa insists that the family stay together and provide mutual support through all their difficulties; if the family can endure, then there are hopes her children will do something more than just survive and improve themselves materially: they may find other values to respect.[24]

Though such problems of adjustment to a new society and culture have been common to all urban immigrant groups, there can be no doubt that Jewish writers have done more than those of any other group to transform that experience into literature. Indeed, with the award of Nobel prizes for Literature to Saul Bellow in 1976 and Isaac Bashevis Singer in 1978, Jewish-American writing has taken its place on a world stage. Of course, by no means all the works, and in some cases very few indeed, of the major Jewish-American authors deal *specifically* with the immigrant experience. But it is true to say that much Jewish-American literature contains the essence of the immigrant experience in its stress upon the individual at odds with the values of the world in which he finds himself. The success of this literature rests upon its awareness that life is difficult and problematical for all men and has always been so. In the twentieth century, however, there are the added strains of alienation related to the pressures of an urban, fragmented society in which man is very small indeed and in which the old sureties of widely accepted value systems no longer exist. Abraham Chapman comments that Jewish-American writers present

> an underlying attitude toward life that derives somehow from the core of the Jewish experience: learning how to live and cope with the continuous expectation of uncertainty, contradictions, the unpredictable, the unanticipated and the unfathomable, with the realization that adversity, trouble, grief, and sorrows, all embodied in the Yiddish word *tsuris*, are the normal conditions of life. Calamities are not the end of the world but realities in the struggle for survival.[25]

Despite this rather pessimistic description, this literature also contains a strongly optimistic note, a feeling that while the world may be a difficult place, man's task is to attempt to understand his role in it and, more importantly, to have compassion for the difficulties of his fellow men who are in the same position as he. Perhaps this attitude is best summed up in a remark attributed to the former Israeli prime minister Golda Meir: "Pessimism is a luxury which a Jew has never been able to afford."

The majority of Jews in America today are descended from poor and religiously orthodox Russian and East European Jews who fled from harshly restrictive laws and pogroms after 1880 and settled in American cities, particularly New York. They had been preceded by much smaller groups of more cosmopolitan German-speaking Jews, who began arriving around 1836, and by Portugese and Spanish Jews, who began entering America after 1654. Large numbers of these German-speaking and 'Sephardic' Jews were traders, with many of the former moving around the country and advancing from peddling to the ownership of large department stores or becoming financiers and entrepreneurs. However, as they comprised the largest migration of Jews in history, it is the Russian and East European Jews who provided most of the inspiration and the authors for the development of Jewish-American literature.

The Earlier Jewish-American Writers

One touchingly expressive member of the "huddled masses" was Mary Antin, who arrived in Boston in 1891 from Polotzk, in the Russian Pale of Settlement. Her autobiography *The Promised Land* (1912) is a moving document of the significance of America to one who experienced at first hand the persecution of Jews in Russia and their freedom in the United States. Jews could not leave the area known as the "Pale" in order to live in the rest of Russia — they were, in fact, prisoners in a part of the country not large enough to provide a living for them. They were taxed far beyond the level of their gentile neighbours and ran the risk of being forced into the Czar's army and of being forcibly baptized. She resigned herself to being spat upon by a gentile boy, since there was nothing she could do about it. Within this "exile," however, she notes that "A poor scholar would be preferred in the marriage market to a rich ignoramus. In the phrase of our grandmothers, a boy stuffed with learning was worth more than a girl stuffed with bank notes." This devotion to learning was the most important asset which the Jews brought to the New World, for it assured their success in a free society. For her father, education for his children was "the essence of American opportunity, the treasure that no thief would touch, not even misfortune or poverty."[26]

Shortly after arriving in the United States, Mary is sent to the free public school. It opens up an entirely new world to her, including a profound love for America. She even wins praise for a poem about George Washington, which is printed in a local newspaper to the elation of her parents. The family's Americanization rapidly accelerates, her father relinquishing orthodox religious practices as he feels they they will hamper the assimilation process. The solid base of accepted values is removed, and the parents learn from the children what American mores are, even as their own authority as parents is undermined. Perhaps the price for Americanization is too high, but Antin believes that even immigrant parents found some joy in the process as they saw their children becoming real Americans.

What America meant to her, Mary Antin thought it also meant to immigrant Jews as a whole. In her Introduction, she wrote:

Although I have written a genuine personal memoir, I believe that its chief interest lies in the fact that it is illustrative of scores of unwritten lives. I am only one of many whose fate it has been to live a page of modern history. We are the strands of the cable that binds the Old World to the New.[27]

Like Hans Mattson, Mary Antin saw herself as a representative of her people. Both authors saw the countries in which they were born as places of injustice and America as a truly 'promised land.' The greater harshness which Antin experienced in Russia may help explain the more emotional approach which she takes in her autobiography as compared to Mattson's "plain recital" of his life. America meant opportunity to Mattson; it meant life itself to Antin along with opportunity. Both were successes in the United States: the many failures by definition tended not to get their autobiographies published!

A somewhat less affirmative attitude was expressed by Abraham Cahan, who arrived in America from Vilna in 1882 and, in that year, gave the first socialist lecture in Yiddish in the United States. He had an enormous influence upon Russian and East European Jews through his editorship of *The Jewish Daily Forward*, which became the most important of many Yiddish language newspapers in the United States and provided an important aid to the immigrant Jewish population in its attempt to understand and become a part of the new country. While Cahan's short stories[28] highlight the problems of the immigrant and depict the process of Americanization, his major work is undoubtedly *The Rise of David Levinsky* (1917), a classic novel of the Jewish immigrant experience.

Like Mary Antin, Cahan describes the harsh conditions under which Jews lived in Russia, in this case in the fictional town of Antomir. David Levinsky's mother is murdered by anti-Semites, and the period around 1881 with its virulent anti-Jewishness is described, as is the great poverty of most Jews. Levinsky is a budding Talmudic scholar but is attracted by secular books and un-Jewish thoughts even before arriving in America. When he considers going to America, he is told that it is a country in which Jews cease to be observant of the commandments, but he believes that it is possible to be a good Jew there. This is shown, in his case, to be a vain hope. Levinsky becomes a clothing manufacturer, employs cheap labour to increase his profits, and avoids union regulations. He is violently anti-socialist, and little survives in the wealthy cloak manufacturer of the poor scholar from Europe, who at least had tried to preserve his sense of ethics.

Cahan saw himself as a Realist and consciously dedicated himself and his work to the overthrow of the romantic "Genteel Tradition." In Cahan's opinion, American capitalism had created an unjust and corrupt society. He therefore believed that the best way to further the ends of socialism was to depict society as it was. In 1913, when *The Rise of David Levinsky* was published, literature of a sentimental nature was still enormously popular. Despite the writings of the Naturalists, the American public was not interested in fiction which presented the real problems of an industrial society.

The Rise of David Levinsky was based upon a series of articles entitled "The Autobiography of an American Jew," which Cahan published in *McClure's Magazine*. Jules Chametzky comments that Cahan knew well the type of businessman portrayed in Levinsky; he adds: "That book, as John Higham perceptively notes, combines the distinctly American theme of success with a Jewish subject-matter and a Russian artistic sensibility. Into it Cahan put all of his rich experience, all he had learned about life and writing."[29] Unfortunately, Cahan's style remains flat and often unconvincing because Levinsky, his narrator, never manages to communicate a sense of true emotional reaction even when we suspect that he must be feeling deeply. He relates rather than dramatizes, in a rather distant, rhetorical style.

The comments of Hector St. John de Crèvecoeur, relevant as always to the American immigrant experience, certainly apply to David Levinsky in particular:

> Crèvecoeur talks about "the new man" who leaves "behind him all his ancient prejudices and manners" in order to receive "new ones from the new mode of life he has embraced." In achieving the language and customs of the new land, Levinsky gives up, chiefly, his mother-tongue and the older Jewish values.[30]

In *The Rise of David Levinsky*, Abraham Cahan depicts not only the intense love for America which those immigrants who are successful there feel but also the sense of loss which many of them, whether or not they are successful, experience. The final paragraph of the novel presents David Levinsky bemoaning his lost past: "I cannot escape from my old self. My past and my present do not comport well. David, the poor lad swinging over a Talmud volume at the Preacher's Synagogue, seems to have more in common with my inner identity than David Levinsky, the well-known cloak-manufacturer."[31] We must take Cahan's word for this as he never depicts this state of mind through Levinsky's actions. Nonetheless, the novel provides both a fascinating history of the New York garment industry in the decades around the turn of the century and a realistic account of the Americanization of a Russian Jew.

By contrast, it was the barriers to assimilation that impressed Ludwig Lewisohn, who was born in Germany and arrived in the United States in 1890, at the age of seven. German Jews had been the most assimilated Jews in Europe, developing a form of worship, Reform Judaism, which had eliminated those differences in dress, liturgy, and language which so separated Jews visibly from their gentile neighbours in some other European countries. They were modernists rather than traditionalists. Lewisohn experienced a deep sense of frustration upon discovering that subtle restrictions and social attitudes against Jews existed in the United States. Disenchanted with the possibilities for assimilation, he became convinced that the only way in which Jews could remain well-adjusted individuals was to return to a sense of Jewish peoplehood. He wrote of his disappointment in America in *Up Stream* (1922) and to greater effect in his best work, *The Island Within* (1928).

Carrying work home, c.1910. Another fine photograph of the Lower East Side, in this case by an unknown photographer.

The Island Within is concerned with the psychological effects of anti-Jewishness on first and second-generation American Jews. Although the first fifth of the book is set in Europe, it is merely preparation for the issue of assimilation which occurs in the main body of the work. The protagonist is Arthur Levy, who assumes that he is as American as the next fellow, but an awareness of his Jewish origins is slowly impressed upon him from without. However, because he has not been brought up as a Jew, he does not know how Jews behave, and lacking any real identity he loses all confidence in himself. He wonders, "How was it that, before they went to school, always and always, as far back as the awakening of consciousness, the children knew that they were Jews? . . . There was in the house no visible symbol of religion and of race." He wonders how both he and his sister have developed the awareness of being Jews, but the answer is not difficult to find — non-Jews have not let them forget who they are.

Arthur begins to question the nature of Jewishness, as in conversation with his friend:

> "Can we be less Jewish than we are?" Arthur asked. "Isn't it only that we're not honest about it? What is specifically Jewish about you and me?"
>
> Joe's eyes were suddenly veiled by their deepest melancholy.
>
> "I don't know. I'll be damned if I know. And yet . . . Oh, for Christ's sake let's talk about something else. I'm sick of it."

He looks at this father and notices how Jewish he looks, then realizes how absurd this is: "Fancy an Irish-American boy saying to himself:

How Irish my father looks!" Thus, from its not being an issue, Arthur's Jewishness becomes the central factor in his life in his attempts to come to grips with American ideas of equality for all. He starts moving more and more toward the idea that Jews must preserve their sense of peoplehood if they are to remain whole and not become self-hating through doomed attempts at gaining access to gentile society. Ironically, he finally appreciates his father's point of view that people should stay with their own kind, that there is a limit to how far Jews can assimilate into American society.[32]

The period in which the major portion of this novel is set, the late nineteenth and early twentieth centuries, was a time when there was resistance to the rise of Jews in American society, first the German and then the East European and Russian. Lewisohn experienced great difficulty in obtaining a university post, simply because he was Jewish. Much of *The Island Within* is semi-autobiographical and traces Lewisohn's own increasing concern with Jewish consciousness. Like Lewisohn, other second-generation American Jews continued to experience discrimination and wrote from their preoccupation with the marginal status they felt their Jewishness conferred on them; but they also developed larger, more socially aware concerns.

The poverty and hardship on the Lower East Side of Manhattan were extreme, as many fine photographs demonstrate. Not that the Jews living there were not accustomed to poverty, but in Europe they had had cohesive communities and a set of shared beliefs which had helped to cushion their problems; in America the cohesiveness of the communities was nothing like it had been in Europe, and orthodox beliefs tended to disappear under the pressures of earning a living and of Americanization. One not uncommon reaction of second-generation Jews, especially in New York and Chicago, was to turn to a new orthodoxy to help them explain and confront their situation: that of the Communist Party. Jews made a significant and disproportionate contribution to its leadership and activists in general; they also served as many of its most articulate spokesman and ideologues, using social realist fiction for political purposes. One of the best examples of this genre — and a vivid description of the seamy side of immigrant East Side life — is found in Michael Gold's autobiographical novel *Jews Without Money* (1930).

Gold was born Irwin Granich, in 1893, of Roumanian Jewish parents, on the Lower East Side. To Gold, Jewish messianism came to mean communism, and he became editor of *The New Masses* in 1928. *Jews Without Money* depicts the experiences which led Gold along this path. He points out that pious Jews had to tolerate the prostitutes and sweat-shops because they had no choice. The severe overcrowding of a big city ghetto made any waste bit of land a valuable playground, despite the possible presence of "perverts, cokefiends, kidnapers [sic], firebugs, Jack the Rippers." The East River provided swimming facilities:

> Our East River is a sun-spangled open sewer running with oily scum and garbage. It should be underground, like a sewer . . . . Often while swimming I had to push dead swollen dogs and vegetables from my face. In our set it was considered humor to slyly paddle ordure at another boy when he was swimming.

In this sort of environment, there were "Thousands of tuberculars and paralytics; a vast anemia and hunger; a world of feebleness and of stomachs, livers, and lungs rotting away. Babies groaning and dying in thousands: insomnia — worry." Gold presents anti-union employers such as David Levinsky as the arch-enemies of humanity. A young doctor tells a patient that no medicine can cure him: "You slave too many hours in your lousy sweatshop; you need food and rest, brother. That's what's wrong with you! Join a labour union."

The doctor's advice is the sort that Gold took to heart, and then took further. It was not just the formation of unions which was important, but the transformation of the entire capitalist system. Gold recounts his father's bitterness at his own failure to succeed: there is no gold in the streets; he has to work extremely hard just to make a living and comes to believe that money is everything in America. "It is all useless. A curse on Columbus! A curse on America, the thief! It is a land where the lice make fortunes, and the good men starve!"[33]

The book was the first important work of proletarian literature in the United States, a piece of social protest which at the very end provided an answer to the East Side's problems in a worker's revolution. It is not a great work of art, being more of a collection of remembered scenes interlaced with authorial comment. But it certainly possesses the ring of truth to observed reality, and it reflected contemporary Jewish concern with problems of class and status. But Jews in the thirties, for all their involvement in proletarian problems, did produce a number of works that transcend a particular time and achieve a true artistic success — most notably, Henry Roth's *Call it Sleep* (1934).

In Leslie Fiedler's opinion, *Call it Sleep* is "the best single book by a Jew about Jewishness written by an American, certainly through the thirties and perhaps ever."[34] While one can argue about whether the novel is concerned with 'Jewishness' as such, its artistic quality is unquestionable. Like *Jews Without Money*, *Call it Sleep* is concerned with poor immigrant Jews, but it would not be entirely correct to refer to it as a "proletarian novel." It is, if anything, a psychological novel about the adjustment needed to cope with his father and a new environment by a six to eight-year-old boy. It was strongly criticized by the Communist press for not being committed enough to social revolution, but that may well be the reason why it achieved the artistry it did: Roth created a work of art, not a polemic. He later found himself pulled in different directions: art for art's sake or literature as a means to further social justice — he has not yet completed another novel.

The novel is semi-autobiographical and presents the immigrant experience as an important element in David Shearl's psychic problems. In the Prologue, Roth describes the arrival of David and his mother in America. David is dressed in his European clothes, and his father cannot bear to be thought a "greenhorn," to be mocked. He throws the boy's blue straw hat into the bay, symbolically throwing off a European attachment. The entire arrival scene is presented not with hopefulness but with despondency. Genya comments that "this is the Golden Land," but Albert just grunts and says nothing. Even the Statue of Liberty is presented as a frightening object.

They go to the Brownsville section of Brooklyn to live, later moving to Manhattan's Lower East Side. Henry Roth himself was born in Galicia in 1906 and, like David Shearl, came to the United States with his mother in order to join his father. As an immigrant child, Roth enjoyed a certain amount of security in the Jewish Lower East Side, but lost it when the family moved to Harlem and he had to face Irish anti-Semitism. He says that he changed his depiction of the East Side in *Call it Sleep* to one far more negative than he had, in fact, found it: "*Call it Sleep* is set in the East Side, but it violates the truth about what the East Side was like back then . . . . In reality, I took the violent environment of Harlem — where we lived from 1914 to 1928 — and projected it back onto the East Side." For David, the streets of the East Side are threatening because of gangs of gentile youths, and his apartment dangerous because of his unpredictable, paranoid father, who is not certain that David is his own child. The 'truth' of *Call it Sleep* is, as in Willa Cather's depiction of immigrants in Nebraska, an artistic truth. Roth said later. "I was working with characters, situations and events that had in part been taken from life, but which I molded to give expression to what was oppressing me. To a considerable extent I was drawing on the unconscious to give shape to remembered reality."[35]

Roth presents the tensions between the various cultures. A Jew and an Italian are seen hurling epithets at each other; gentile gangs attack David because he is a Jew. One also sees the loss of religious life amongst the second-generation Jews, who grow up on the streets and have no use for the *cheder* [Hebrew school]. One cannot say that Albert Shearl's problems are due solely to his uprooting and the problems inherent in adjusting to a new society. Albert's problems are more

"Knee-pants at forty-five cents a dozen — a Ludlow Street sweater's shop."
This photograph of working conditions on the Lower East Side was taken by
Jacob Riis and appeared in his book How The Other Half Lives
(New York, 1890).

deeply embedded. But certainly part of his difficulty lies in the
necessity of coming to grips with a new urban society, which makes far
different demands on him than did his native Austria, where he lived
in the countryside.

Bertha, Genya's sister, has mixed reactions to America. On the one
hand, she loves the clothes and the excitement. Albert points out that
America requires more effort than it is worth, but Bertha comments,
in her usual colourful language: "True I work like a horse and I stink
like one with my own sweat. But there's life here, isn't there! There's a
stir here always . . . . Veljish [back in Austria] was still as a fart in
company. Who could endure it?" Yet, at other times she bemoans her
fate: "Why did I ever set foot on this stinking land? Why did I ever
come here? Ten hours a day in a smothering shop — paper flowers!
Rag flowers! Ten long hours, afraid to pee too often because the
foreman might think I was shirking." America provided an escape
from persecution in Europe, but for most first-generation Jewish
immigrants the streets were not paved with gold.

The urban immigrant experience was made much harsher for those whose native language was not English. Until he could understand English and make himself understood, an immigrant was at a severe disadvantage in the New World. Neither Genya nor Bertha can speak English, only Yiddish. Albert's English is extremely limited, as can be seen when he tries to communicate with a policeman at the end of the novel, "My sawn. Mine. Yes. Awld eight. Eight en' — en' vun mawnt'. He vas bawn in —." David speaks Yiddish in the house and a mixture of broken English with Yiddish inflections in the street. The speech patterns of the gentile children in the streets and of the neighbours are also suggested. Influenced by James Joyce, Roth also uses stream-of-consciousness, which he presents through a choppy sentence structure. He shows great skill in his presentation of these various dialects and in his general command of literary technique.[36]

Call it Sleep is a major American novel both for its artistic quality and for its sensitivity in presenting the fears and problems of a Jewish immigrant child. In this way the novel marked a move away from social concern and group awareness towards an obsession with the self, with the problems of the individual surrounded by an unfriendly, impersonal society to which he or she has difficulty relating. This was to be a major feature of Jewish-American writing after World War II, though there have remained some writers concerned above all with essentially Jewish problems.

The Jewish-American Novel since 1945

Chaim Potok is that rarity amongst Jewish-American authors, a writer who sees orthodox Judaism as relevant and necessary in the twentieth century. He is a rabbi, and his five novels to date each stress moral and religious themes. His first and arguably best novel, *The Chosen* (1967), is concerned with Russian and East European Hasidic Jews, most of whom are immigrants. Potok reflects reality when he presents this group as not being interested in assimilating into American society. Quite the contrary: their goal is to recreate the religious and social forms in America which had existed in Europe. Unlike those individuals, Jewish or not, who began assimilating into American society as soon as possible, the Hasidic characters in *The Chosen* do their best to isolate themselves, in Brooklyn, from the rest of America. Indeed, the basic conflict in the novel revolves about whether Danny Saunders, the genius son of the sage-like leader of a particular Hasidic group, will refuse to take on the inherited role of "rebbe" (or rabbi) after his father or leave the group and move out into the non-Hasidic world.

Potok's style combines weak dialogue, in which he fails to individualize his characters, with intrusive though interesting accounts of Jewish history and religious lore. *The Chosen*, like his other novels, works because of his story-telling ability and the fact that his characters are still interesting as people despite the technical weakness in his presentation of them. Also, they fulfil certain concepts inherent in the American dream — concepts which are at the root of the immigrants' ideal America in that

> the story is played out by an improbable but possible "only in America" cast of Hasidic and orthodox Jews, who demonstrate that people can still make good through hard work, and that severe difficulties can be overcome by pluck, integrity, and dedication. At the story's end the novel's two young heroes are about to realize the reward they have earned: a limitless future. In sum, *The Chosen* can be interpreted from this standpoint as an assertion of peculiarly American optimism and social idealism. Very simply, it says Yes.[37]

As a novel, then, *The Chosen* is not entirely successful, but as a social document, a work which encapsulates some of the problems of an immigrant group having beliefs and practices which are very different from those of the majority society and battling with the problem of assimilation, the book has much to recommend it. Potok seeks to demonstrate that this group's values fit them for success in America, in that both the extreme and somewhat less extreme levels of Jewish orthodoxy inculcate honesty, loyalty and respect for hard work and learning. Thus, the novel presents an ideological defence of the relevance of orthodox Judaism to modern, secular American life as well as an accurate picture of the physical and social aspects of a particular group of people in a particular place and time.

In *The Chosen* Potok stresses religious and cultural reasons for his characters' difficulties in feeling at peace in the American environment; but for most post-Second World War Jewish writers there is another experience, besides immigration, which lends them a critical distance from the everyday routines of American life: the Holocaust. In Isaac Bashevis Singer's novel *Enemies: A Love Story* (1972) and Edward Lewis Wallant's *The Pawnbroker* (1961), the protagonists' difficulties stem from their being haunted by memories of Nazi persecution. The heroes are both Jewish immigrants among the 150,000 who managed to drag themselves to America after World War II with little more baggage than their lives. Both are haunted men for whom America means not so much freedom as a place where they can be left alone to try to forget — unsuccessfully. Singer's Herman Broder was never in a concentration camp, but spent the war years in Europe hiding and being hunted. He walks about Brooklyn remembering the hayloft in Lipsk where he eluded the Nazis, but he is still looking for hiding places in case the Nazis come to Brooklyn to hunt him there. His frenetic sexual life confirms his inability to form a human relationship. Wallant's Sol Nazerman has succeeded in stifling all human emotion in his pawnshop in Harlem. But as the anniversary of the death of his family in the camps approaches, he finds that memories which he thought he had thoroughly repressed begin to come to consciousness again. As in his other three novels, Wallant slowly and agonizingly moves the protagonist to a point where he can rejoin the human race, where he can feel for his suffering fellow man again. In both of these novels the immigrant experience is peculiarly a nightmare; the protagonists live in their memories more than in an actual place called America.

Singer has published a number of short stories which contain characters who are immigrants in the United States. However, because of his orientation to Eastern European myths and Judaic practices, these tales are often very similar to those set in *shtetls* (or Jewish villages) in Europe in terms of their characterization, dialogue, and atmosphere. When he uses an American setting, the tales are rarely as satisfying as those with an Eastern European milieu. A brilliant writer, Singer's best work does not concern the immigrant experience in America but is rooted in a European context.[38]

Unlike Singer, the major writers of Jewish-American literature since World War II — Saul Bellow, Bernard Malamud, and Philip Roth — are primarily concerned with presenting various aspects of American life. Though none can be said to be overwhelmingly concerned with the immigrant experience, each presents aspects of it in various novels and short stories. It is, of course, very much the case that the further away from the era of large-scale immigration one moves, the less direct concern there is with the immigrant and the more with the problems of ethnicity in later generations. These problems, however, are not dissimilar from those faced by newly arrived immigrants in terms of Jewish identity and assimilation. Most often the problems of physical survival — jobs and money — have been solved, but the problem of the nature of an individual's Jewishness in a society which grants equality of opportunity has not.

In Saul Bellow's novel, *Mr. Sammler's Planet* (1970), the protagonist has, like Sol Nazerman and Herman Broder, escaped from the Nazis — but only barely. Artur Sammler, a Polish Jew, has dragged himself out of a mass grave. Like Herman Broder, he spent the war years in hiding, but also was a member of a guerilla band for a time. Before the war he was a journalist in London. Now he is living in New York City, and unlike Sol Nazerman his experiences have not made him indifferent to the society around him — quite the contrary. Sammler delivers a series of criticisms of American society in the 1960s which stem directly from his European attitudes and experiences: an image of civilized order in Bloomsbury and the falling apart of the civilized world during the war.

With his one good eye (the other smashed by a rifle butt), he views what he perceives as the decay of Western civilization's values. He deplores the youth cult, the new liberal intellectual attack upon what he believes to be true values, the lack of restraint, the self-centredness of people, and the lack of respect for the humanity of others:

> Like many people who had seen the world collapse once, Mr. Sammler entertained the possibility it might collapse twice. He did not agree with refugee friends that this doom was inevitable, but liberal beliefs did not seem capable of self-defence, and you could smell decay. You could see the suicidal impulses of civilization pushing strongly.

Viewed by most of the younger characters as out of touch with contemporary approaches to important issues, Sammler suffers from extreme culture shock. Bellow, Singer, and Wallant all present those protagonists who have survived the Holocaust and arrived as immigrants in America as being peculiarly unable to deal with American society. Only Bellow, however, creates a protagonist who is a vibrant social critic — though stylistically the novel is overburdened by interior monologues and "lectures" presenting this criticism — and who also preserves his faith in mankind despite his recognition of all man's negative aspects: "There are still human qualities. Our weak species fought its fears, our crazy species fought its criminality. We are an animal of genius."[39]

In his earlier novel, *The Victim* (1947), Bellow is concerned with responses to immigration on the part of a 'WASP.' Kirby Allbee believes not only that Asa Leventhal, a second-generation Jewish-American, is responsible for the loss of his job, but that the Jews have taken over New York City from the earlier English Protestant settlers:

> "Do you know, one of my ancestors was Governor Winthrop. Governor Winthrop!" His voice vibrated fiercely; there was a repressed laugh in it . . . . "It's really as if the children of Caliban were running everything . . . . The old breeds are out. The streets are named after them. But what are they themselves? Just remnants."

This resistance to the rise of the Jews from their ghettos to positions of success in American society was resented by many of the older, more settled Americans. As Ludwig Lewisohn's *The Island Within* demonstrated, this resentment often took the form of social exclusion before World War II, though since then the more blatant exclusionary practices against Jews in universities, clubs, hotels, and society at large have disappeared. Allbee is, indeed, a "remnant," but of pre-World War II ethnocentricism.

Now a tramp, Allbee is desperate to show that his fall is not his own fault, that these relative newcomers cannot fully understand the American culture of which he is so integral a part:

> "I saw a book about Thoreau and Emerson by a man named Lipschitz . . . ."
> "What of it?"
> "A name like that?" Allbee said this with great earnestness. "After all, it seems

to me that people of such background simply couldn't understand . . . ."
"Of all the goddamned nonsense!" shouted Leventhal. "Look, I've got things
to attend to."

Although Bellow takes further the issue of how much responsibility
any man has for another, the direct implication of these passages is
that the established group must find a scapegoat for any loss of power
or prestige in order to remove the burden of failure from itself.[40] Thus,
the Jews assume their classic role. Being too successful, they bring
down upon themselves the wrath of those with whom they are
competing.

By contrast, Morris Bober, the protagonist of Bernard Malamud's
novel *The Assistant* (1957), never learned how to compete successfully
in materialistic America. A first-generation Jewish immigrant, he
came to America from Russia with great hopes and found himself
stuck in a poor grocery store. He bemoans his lost youth and
castigates himself for not making the right decisions at the right time.
For Morris "America had become too complicated. One man counted
for nothing. There were too many stores, depressions, anxieties. What
had he escaped to here?" Morris' problem is that his values clash with
those of America. Though he is not a religious Jew, he believes that all
men are responsible for the welfare of others; he believes in the Jewish
law: "This means to do what is right, to be honest, to be good. This
means to other people." At Morris' funeral, the rabbi reiterates the
truth of the dead grocer's beliefs. Unfortunately, these are not the
values which make for success in the United States, and by American
(and his wife's) standards Morris is a failure.[41]

Walter Shear points out that "In *The Assistant* two cultures, the
Jewish tradition and the American heritage (representing the wisdom
of the old world and the practical knowledge of the new), collide and
to some degree synthesize to provide a texture of social documentation which is manifested in a realistic aesthetic."[42] The sense of the
Old World is conveyed through Morris' heavy Yiddish inflections,
which are replete with an ironic humorous tone:

"You should sell long ago the store," she remarked after a minute.
"When the store was good, who wanted to sell? After came bad times, who
wanted to buy?"

The basis of this style "owes something to the wile of Yiddish folklore,
the ambiguous irony of the Jewish joke. Pain twisted into humor
twists humor back into pain."[43] There is a bitter-sweet quality of hope
encased in pain in this style, and the ultimate paradox of the novel lies
in the fact that Morris' failure in materialistic America is the cause of
his success as a human being. Because he refuses to forsake high
standards of honesty and goodness, he cannot succeed in the timeless,
depressed neighbourhood where fate has placed him. The novel
documents not only the life and death of a good man and the effect for

good which he has upon another failure by New World standards, but also the tension between certain Old and New World values and the culture shock which many immigrants had to endure. Most Jewish-American fiction would endorse Malamud's pessimistic conclusion on this score rather than Potok's exceptionally affirmative attitude.[44]

A man who is not a failure by American standards is Ben Patimkin, in Philip Roth's novella *Goodbye, Columbus* (1959). He has left the area of first settlement in Newark, the area to which his European-born parents had come, and made it to wealthy Short Hills. Neil Klugman, the young protagonist, relates some of the history of the place: "The neighborhood had changed: the old Jews like my grandparents had struggled and died, and their offspring had struggled and prospered, and moved further and further west . . . . Now, in fact, the Negroes were making the same migration, following the steps of the Jews." Unlike Morris Bober, Ben is willing to be a bit of a "thief" in order to succeed — and America rewards him.

The novella concerns a choice amongst values: the materialism of the Patimkins, living on the cool heights of Short Hills, as compared to a somewhat obscure set of non-materialistic, more human values held or aspired to by the protagonist, Neil Klugman. Neil is living with his Aunt Gladys, a first-generation immigrant who has not escaped Newark, but he is sexually drawn to Brenda Patimkin and, initially at least, to her lifestyle. At the very beginning of the novella Roth makes the difference between these two generations clear. The streets of Short Hills are named after eastern colleges, and as he drives through them to meet Brenda, Neil muses:

> I thought of my Aunt Gladys and Uncle Max sharing a Mounds bar in the cindery darkness of their alley, on beach chairs, each cool breeze sweet to them as the promise of after life, and after a while I rolled onto the gravel roads of the small park where Brenda was playing tennis.

The differences are great, but the elder Patimkins still retain their old Newark furniture in the attic, an old refrigerator (now full of fruit), and a somewhat moralistic preference for good eaters and strong fabrics in clothes. It is almost as though, as Brenda puts it in talking of her mother," Money is a waste for her. She doesn't even know how to enjoy it. She still thinks we live in Newark."[45]

Although Roth's depiction of the conflict between the American success ethic and more human values clearly stresses, as did Mala-mud in *The Assistant*, the danger of the loss of the more basic values as American materialism takes over, some critics feel that he is dishonest in his presentation of the characters. Certainly the Patimkins and Aunt Gladys, like the assimilated Jews of Woodenton in his story "Eli, the Fanatic,"[46] are not presented as having any real insight into the deeper issues which their actions imply; at times they become mere caricatures. Yet, the problem of having to contend with the "swamp of prosperity," to use Saul Bellow's phrase, is vividly presented in *Goodbye, Columbus*. The protagonist finally rejects it, but what, as a third-generation American Jew, he is left with remains in doubt.

These works represent only a small sample of the scores of works which Jewish-Americans have produced. Why have they been so prolific? First, Jews have long been known as "the people of the book," not only for their devotion to the Old Testament but because of the great value which they have always placed upon sheer literacy, if only for males and only in Hebrew and Yiddish. The poorest European ghetto might manage to have its Talmud students, who would be supported by the community to study the ancient commentaries of great sages. Wives would work so that their husbands could study the holy books. As Mary Antin's autobiography showed, scholarship was held in extremely high regard, and it was but a short step from the devotion to religious texts to a similar devotion to secular literature, as can be seen in the experience of David Levinsky. In a broader sense this explains, in part, the great success of Jews entering the professions.

Second, Jews found that they had an audience. Originally it was a Yiddish-speaking one, and then became English-speaking. Jews are great consumers of books (Israel has one of the highest per capita purchase of books in the world), and a Jewish writer or journalist writing in New York around the turn of the century (like Abraham Cahan) knew that he had readers. As the United States became more and more urban, non-Jews began finding that some Jewish writers were speaking for them as well as for Jews. Jews were the experts on 'marginality,' which became an increasingly important topic in the twentieth century; Jews were experts on urban life and its problems, again becoming cultural spokesman for all Americans, of whatever ethnic origin, who felt ill at ease in the new urban American culture. Thus, the Jewish writer's audience grew rapidly.

Other immigrant groups had possessed some interest in literary matters, but none had the combination of centuries of great respect for words and learning, centuries of experience as marginal outsiders, a large segment with long experience in cities, and a fervent messianic hope which could be transmuted into optimism for the future in spite of the nature of the present reality. These elements made the Jews ideal interpreters of the twentieth-century American experience.

4: Literature and Immigrants

The writings over which this survey has glanced offer many realistic glimpses of the manners, the speech, the ethnic prejudices, the exotic imagination of Scandinavian or Jewish immigrants as they confront, adapt, succumb to or are corrupted or strengthened by the American environments, frontier or urban, into which their uprooting had thrown them. These works usually depicted *transitional* modes of life and even employed (with honourable exceptions like the traditionalist Singer) transitional modes of literary expression, halfway between their own traditions and those of the host society. This is clear in their adaptation of speech patterns and mannerisms from languages other than American English, and their use of imported folk-naivety and folk-wisdom for stereotyping characters. Traditional themes persisted, too, in the form of Christian heroism or Jewish suffering, though, as the mid-twentieth century approached, their characters fitted increasingly well into a noticeably more American landscape.

This literature relating to the immigrant experience, all in all, proved a most welcome injection into the American literary tradition. By the late nineteenth century the traditional currents of American literature no longer represented the mainstream of American experience. The so-called "Genteel Tradition," America's version of British Victorianism, did not adequately reflect the main developments of the time — the settling of the Far Western frontier and the industrialization of the cities. Immigrants were at the heart of these processes, and provided an intricacy of social and cultural mores different from those of native Americans. Thus the subject-matter available to authors concerned with writing a peculiarly *American* literature was increased enormously, and the work of most late nineteenth-century literary Naturalists, whether relating to farm or factory, responded to the plight of people who may not have been presented as immigrants but who were often probably recent arrivals in the United States. Moreover, immigrant writers themselves often consciously worked for a shift in the direction of American culture, as was most obvious in the socially conscious and politically aware young Jewish socialist writers who became so prominent during the depression of the 1930s. Whereas the writers of, say, the expatriate tradition had represented an educated, literate elite, able to travel abroad and experience an older, fuller, more confident culture, the writers who portrayed the immigrant experience marked a 'proletarianizing' influence which in some ways reflected more accurately what was happening in the United States itself.[47]

After World War II, however, immigrant literature lost much of its distinctiveness. Most Scandinavian writing by the 1950s seemed to become just another variation of American regional literature, which no doubt reflected the comparative ease with which most North European Protestants were assimilated and began to adopt American cultural perceptions and attitudes. By contrast, American Jews, though they have largely accepted American cultural values, have yet produced major novelists who appear to represent a distinctive tradition. Even so, their preoccupations have ceased to be purely Jewish; instead they have become effective literary spokesmen for educated urban men in contemporary America. There is an obvious compatibility between the witty, sophisticated temperament which marks many modern Jewish fictions and the sense of smart alienation of the bourgeois American intelligentsia — so that the Jewishness of a character like Bellow's Henderson is not a matter of ethnicity or religion but of outlook and personal tone. Some Jewish-American writers have fused older European forms and perceptions with American literary traditions and cultural experience, and the Jewish literary mode has interpenetrated with the American without becoming indistinguishable. In the process it has made American literature more universal, more accessible to other peoples, more significant for modern educated men everywhere.

Guide to Further Reading

There are a number of general works on American immigration, each of which offers a suitable starting point. In *American Immigration* (Chicago: Chicago UP, 1960), Maldwyn A. Jones neatly surveys all aspects of the subject, while his *Destination America* (1976)[3]* concentrates more upon the various immigrant groups and the problems of assimilation. Philip A.M. Taylor's *The Distant Magnet: European Emigration to the U.S.A.* (New York: Harper and Row, 1971) is a carefully documented account of the immigration process from both the European and American vantage points; it is particularly informative about the Atlantic passage, as also is Terry Coleman's lively *Passage to America: A History of Emigrants from Great Britain and Ireland in the Mid-Nineteenth Century* (London: Hutchinson, 1972). Oscar Handlin's *The Uprooted: The Epic Story of the Great Migrations that Made the American People* (1951; rept., Boston: Little, Brown, 1973) is a minor classic, written in a readable, almost novelistic style, which stresses the difficulties of adjusting to America. More recent writing has drawn a less gloomy picture, as notably in Stephan Thernstrom, *The Other Bostonians: Poverty and Progress in the American Metropolis, 1880-1970* (Cambridge, Mass.: Harvard UP, 1973), while Josef J. Barton, *Peasants and Strangers: Italians, Rumanians and Slovaks in an American City, 1890-1950* (Cambridge, Mass.: Harvard UP, 1975) splendidly demonstrates the different patterns of assimilation possible even within the same ethnic group in Cleveland, Ohio. John Higham's *Strangers in the Land* (1955)[29] remains the most impressive analysis of American reactions to mass immigration.

Leonard Dinnerstein et al.'s useful text, *Natives and Strangers: Ethnic Groups and the Building of America* (New York: Oxford UP, 1979), shows the contribution of a large number of immigrant groups throughout American history to the country's economic growth. Carl Wittke's *The Irish in America* (Baton Rouge: Louisiana State UP, 1956) and William V. Shannon's *American Irish* (1963; rev. ed., New York: Collier, 1966) deal with the problems faced after arrival. Joseph Lopreato, *Italian Americans* (New York: Random House, 1970) discusses this group's development and problems with assimilation within America. Charlotte Erickson, *Invisible Immigrants: the Adaptation of English and Scottish Immigrants in Nineteenth-Century America* (London: Weidenfeld and Nicholson, 1972) reveals the tensions even British settlers faced in the nineteenth century. Nathan Glazer and Daniel P. Moynihan, *Beyond the Melting Pot: The Negroes, Puerto Ricans, Jews,*

For full bibliographical details, see the appropriate reference in the Notes, as indicated.

Italians and Irish of New York City (1963; 2nd ed., Cambridge, Mass.: M.I.T. Press, 1970) presents a sociological study of each of these groups.

Maurice Davie includes in his *World Immigration* (New York: Macmillan, 1936) a useful bibliography listing immigrant biographies and fiction. David Bowers presents a series of essays concerned with immigrant and American culture and institutions in *Foreign Influences in American Life* (New York: Peter Smith, 1952). In *The Rediscovery of the Frontier* (New York: Cooper Square, 1970), Percy Boynton discusses various literary aspects of the treatment of the frontier in fiction and includes a chapter on "The Immigrant Pioneer in Fiction."

A useful book on the Scandinavian immigrant in literature is Dorothy Skardal's *The Divided Heart: Scandinavian Immigrant Experience through Literary Sources* (Oslo: Universitetsforlaget, 1974), which follows the implications of its title in terms of social history. Theodore Blegen's *Norwegian Migration to America, 1825-1860* (Northfield: Norwegian American Historical Association, 1931) is a standard work on its subject. For critical comment on O.E. Rölvaag, see Robert Steensma, "Rölvaag and Turner's Frontier Thesis," *North Dakota Quarterly*, **27** (1959), 100-04, which discusses Rölvaag's attitude toward the frontier as "safety valve" and inspiration of democracy. Benjamin Wells discusses the work of H.H. Boyesen in terms of style and theme in his biographical essay, "Hjalmar Hjorth Boyesen," *Sewanee Review*, **4** (1896), 299-311.

An interesting and enjoyable book relating to Swedes is by H. Arnold Barton, ed., *Letters from the Promised Land: Swedes in America, 1840-1914* (Minneapolis: Minnesota UP, 1975), which presents both background and letters. Discussion of the work of Vilhelm Moberg can be found in Gerhard Alexis, "Moberg's Immigrant Trilogy: A Dubious Conclusion," *Scandinavian Studies*, **38** (1966), 20-25, in which he discusses the publisher's inappropriate excisions and changes to the final two Swedish volumes of the tetralogy in order to make them into one English volume and so produce a trilogy.

The quality of the literature produced in America by German-speaking groups was not as high as that of the Scandinavians. Worthy of mention, however, is Austrian Charles Sealsfield (Karl Anton Postl), whose best work (though not concerned with immigrants as such) is a western adventure novel, *The Cabin Book; or Sketches of Life in Texas*, trans. C.F. Mersch (New York: J. Winchester, 1844). An interesting comparison of literary approaches to, among other things, frontier characters can be found in Karl J. Arndt, "The Cooper-Sealsfield Exchange of Criticism," *American Literature*, **15** (1943), 16-24. The Pennsylvania 'Dutch' (a German group who settled in the seventeenth and eighteenth centuries) produced a literature describing their customs. Helen Reimensyder Martin's *Tillie: A Mennonite Maid, A Story of the Pennsylvania Dutch* (1904; rept., Ridgewood, New Jersey: Gregg, 1968) is critical of many of the group's folkways.

A wide variety of Italian-American authors and their works is discussed in Rose Green's useful text, *The Italian-American Novel: A Document of the Interaction of Two Cultures* (Rutherford: Fairleigh Dickinson UP, 1974). The Italians produced several good minor novelists beside Guido D'Agostino[23] and Mario Puzo.[24] Pietro DiDonato, in his autobiographical novel *Christ in Concrete* (New York: Bobbs Merrill, 1939), documents the difficulties of Italian immigrants in the corrupt construction industry. Later novels, *This Woman* (New York: Ballantine Books, 1958) and *Three Circles of Light* (New York: Julian Messner, 1960), depict social and religious themes as they apply to immigrants. In *The River Between* (New York: E.P. Dutton, 1928), Louis Forgione presents the clash between first and second generations in America. John Fante stresses the psychological problems of Italian-Americans in such works as *Wait Until Spring, Bandini* (New York: Stackpole Sons, 1938) and in the stories in *Dago Red* (New York: Viking, 1940).

The most useful single text concerning Jewish life in America is Oscar Handlin's *Adventure in Freedom: Three Hundred Years of Jewish Life in America* (1954; rept., New York: Kennikat, 1971). Nathan Glazer's *American Judaism* (1957; rept., Chicago UP, 1970) presents a short history of Jewish immigration to America and the changes to Jewish life which took place there. Louis Wirth's *The Ghetto* (1928; rept., Chicago: Chicago UP, 1975) describes both the history and the psychological effects of the ghetto upon Jews in Europe and America. A most readable social history is *The American Jews: Portrait of a Split Personality* (New York: Paperback Library, 1969), by James Yaffe. A study combining immigration history and excerpts from first person accounts of experience as an immigrant is Abraham J. Karp, ed., *Golden Door to America: The Jewish Immigrant Experience* (Harmondsworth: Penguin, 1977).

The most useful study concerning Jewish life in its major American centre is Irving Howe's *The Immigrant Jews of New York: 1881 to the Present* (London: Routledge and Kegan Paul, 1976); the American title is *The World of Our Fathers*. Moses Rischin, *The Promised City: New York's Jews, 1870-1914* (Cambridge, Mass.: Harvard UP, 1962) is a much-respected scholarly study. A graphic text dealing with Jews in New York is Allon Schoener's *Portal to America: The Lower East Side* (New York: Holt, Rinehart, Winston, 1967), which contains newspaper items, letters, pictures, as well as authorial comment. Hutchins Hapgood's *The Spirit of the Ghetto* (1902, rept., Cambridge, Mass.:

Belknap Press, 1967) is a classic — but over-selective — look at the Lower East Side by a non-Jew. Jacob Riis is another observer of the slums, whose *How the Other Half Lives* (1890; rept., New York: Dover, 1971) deals with all of the major ethnic groups living on the Lower East Side. Two autobiographies presenting useful insights into the Jewish immigrant experience are Charles Reznikoff's *Family Chronicle* (1929; rept., London: Norton Bailey, 1969), a fascinating account of the experiences of a father, mother, and son in Russia and New York, and Alfred Kazin's *A Walker in the City* (New York: Harcourt, Brace, 1951), tracing the author's movement from Brooklyn to Manhattan.

Each of the following novels contains a depiction of the reaction against the Judaism of their fathers by second-generation American Jews. *Haunch, Paunch and Jowl: An Autobiography* (New York: Garden City Publishing, 1923), by Samuel Ornitz, is the "autobiography" of the protagonist and, like Meyer Levin's *The Old Bunch* (1937; rept., New York: Citadel, 1942), shows this second generation's intense desire for Americanization. In *Summer in Williamsburg* (1934), *Homage to Blenholt* (1936), and *Low Company* (1937), published in one volume as *The Williamsburg Trilogy* (1934-37; rept., New York: Avon, 1972), Daniel Fuchs presents first and second-generation American Jews struggling to succeed. Clifford Odet's play *Awake and Sing* (New York: Modern Library, 1939) is a folk drama of a Jewish-American middle-class family, containing both first and second generations, trying to cope with the Depression. A portrait of an amusing and endearing Jewish immigrant attempting to learn English can be found in *The Education of Hyman Kaplan* (1937; rept., New York: Harcourt, Brace and World, 1965) and *The Return of Hyman Kaplan* (1938; rept., Harmondsworth: Penguin, 1968), by Leo Rosten (pseud. Leonard Q. Ross). A recent *tour de force* of Jewish and other humour seen in terms primarily of second-generation American Jews is Joseph Heller's *Good As Gold* (London: Jonathan Cape, 1979).

The most useful single text of literary criticism of Jewish-American literature which has relevance to the immigrant experience is Allen Guttman's *The Jewish Writer in America: Assimilation and the Crisis of Identity* (New York: Oxford UP, 1971). Also useful because of its stress upon the Jewishness of the literary works but relevant to the immigrant experience as well is Irving Malin's *Jews and Americans* (Carbondale: Southern Illinois UP, 1966) while Bernard Sherman's *The Invention of the Jew: Jewish-American Education Novels, 1916-1964* (New York: Thomas Yoseloff, 1969) stresses novels of initiation in terms of different generations and has a strongly immigrant orientation. Postwar Jewish-American novels are discussed critically in the context of modern fiction as a whole in Stan Smith, *The Comic Self in Post-war American Fiction* (1981), the fifth pamphlet in this series.

Notes

1. Hector St. John de Crèvecoeur, *Letters From an American Farmer* (1782; rept., London: J.M. Dent, 1962), p. 43.

2. Henry Seidel Canby et al., "Address to the Reader," in R.E. Spiller et al., eds., *Literary History of the United States,* 3rd rev. edn. (1946; rept., New York: Macmillan, 1965), pp. xx-xxi.

3. Maldwyn A. Jones, *Destination America* (1976; rept., Glasgow: Fontana, 1977), p. 98.

4. Sophus K. Winther, "Moberg and a New Genre for the Emigrant Novel," *Scandinavian Studies,* **34** (1962), 172.

5. O.E. Rölvaag, *Giants in the Earth,* trans. L. Colcord and the author (1927; rept., New York: A.L. Burt, 1929), pp. 212, 249.

6. Vilhelm Moberg, *The Emigrants,* trans. G. Lannestock (Stockholm: Albert Bonniers Forlag, 1951), pp. 154, 186.

7. Joseph E. Baker, "Western Man Against Nature: *Giants in the Earth,*" *College English,* **4** (1942), 24, 19.

8. Philip Holmes, *Vilhelm Moberg: Utvandrarna* (Hull: Studies in Swedish Literature, 1976), pp. 26-27. See also idem, *Vilhelm Moberg* (Boston: Twayne, 1980).

9. Gerhard Alexis, "Sweden to Minnesota: Vilhelm Moberg's Fictional Reconstruction," *American Quarterly,* **18** (1966), 87.

10. O.E. Rölvaag, pp. 297-98.

11. Vernon Louis Parrington, *Main Currents of American Thought* (1927; rept., New York: Harcourt, Brace and World, 1958), vol. 3, pp. 393, 387.

12. Julius Olson, "Rölvaag's Novels of Norwegian Pioneer Life in the Dakotas," *Scandinavian Studies and Notes,* **9** (1926), 48.

13. Hjalmar Hjorth Boyesen, *Falconberg* (1878; rept., New York: Charles Scribner's Sons, 1899), p. 23.

14. Hans Mattson, *Reminiscences: The Story of an Emigrant* (St. Paul: D.D. Merrill, 1892), pp. i, 311.

15. George L. White, Jr., "H.H. Boyesen: A Note on Immigration," *American Literature,* **13** (1942), 366; Carl Wittke, "Melting Pot Literature," *College English,* **7** (1945-46), 193.

16. Philip Gerber, *Willa Cather* (Boston: Twayne, 1975), p. 21.

17. David Daiches, *Willa Cather: A Critical Introduction* (Ithaca; N.Y.: Cornell UP, 1951), p. 28.

18. Willa Cather, *The Song of the Lark,* new rev. edn. (1915; rept., Boston: Houghton Mifflin, 1937), p. vi.

19. Willa Cather, *My Ántonia* (1918; rept., London: Hamish Hamilton, 1962), p. 353.

20. H.L. Mencken, "Four Reviews," and Granville Hicks, "The Case Against Willa Cather," both in James Schroeter, ed., *Willa Cather and Her Critics* (Ithaca, N.Y.: Cornell UP, 1967), pp. 9, 141.

21. T.K. Whipple, "Willa Cather," ibid., p. 40. See also Edward and Lillian Bloom's useful *Willa Cather's Gift of Sympathy* (Carbondale: Southern Illinois UP, 1962) and James Woodress's excellent *Willa Cather: Her Life and Art* (New York: Western Publishing, 1970).

22. James T. Farrell, *Young Lonigan* (1932), *The Young Manhood of Studs Lonigan* (1934), and *Judgment Day* (1935); published in one volume as *Studs Lonigan* (rept., New York: Avon, 1977).

23. Guido D'Agostino, *Olives on the Apple Tree* (New York: Doubleday, Doran, 1940), pp. 26, 294.

24. Mario Puzo, *The Fortunate Pilgrim* (New York: Atheneum, 1964), p. 77. See also *The Godfather* (New York: G.P. Putnam's Sons, 1969).

25. Abraham Chapman, ed., *Jewish-American Literature: An Anthology* (New York: New American Library, 1974), pp. xlvii – xlviii.

26. Mary Antin, *The Promised Land* (Boston: Houghton Mifflin, 1912), pp. 37, 186.

27. Ibid., p. xiii.

28. Abraham Cahan, *Yekl and the Imported Bridegroom and Other Stories of the New York Ghetto* (rept., New York: Dover, 1970). This volume contains the novella *Yekl* (1896) and five of Cahan's stories.

29. Jules Chametzky, *From the Ghetto: The Fiction of Abraham Cahan* (Amherst: Massachusetts UP, 1977), p. 128. See also John Higham, *Strangers In The Land: Patterns of American Nativism, 1860-1925* (New Brunswick, N.J.: Rutgers UP, 1955).

30. Chametzky, p. 142.

31. Abraham Cahan, *The Rise of David Levinsky*, introd. by J. Higham (1917; rept., New York: Harper and Row, 1966), p.530.

32. Ludwig Lewisohn, *The Island Within* (New York: Harper and Brothers, 1928), pp. 103, 147, 148.

33. Michael Gold, *Jews Without Money* (1930; rept., New York: Avon, 1972), pp. 39, 24, 162, 168, 79.

34. Leslie Fiedler, "The Jew in the American Novel," in his *To the Gentiles* (New York: Stein and Day, 1972), p. 96.

35. David Bronsen, "A Conversation With Henry Roth," *Partisan Review*, **2** (1969), pp. 267, 268.

36. Henry Roth, *Call it Sleep* (1934; rept., New York: Avon, 1965), pp. 153, 158, 437.

37. Sheldon Grebstein, "The Phenomenon of the Really Jewish Best Seller: Potok's *The Chosen*," *Studies in American Jewish Literature*, **1** (1975), 25; Chaim Potok, *The Chosen* (New York: Simon and Schuster, 1967). See also Robert H. Fossum and John K. Roth, *The American Dream* (1981), the sixth pamphlet in this series.

38. Isaac Bashevis Singer, *Enemies: A Love Story* (1972; rept., Harmondsworth: Penguin, 1977); Edward Lewis Wallant, *The Pawnbroker* (1961; rept., New York: Manor, 1973).

39. Saul Bellow, *Mr. Sammler's Planet* (New York: Viking, 1970), pp. 37, 308.

40. Saul Bellow, *The Victim* (1947; rept., Harmondsworth: Penguin, 1971), pp. 121, 122.

41. Bernard Malamud, *The Assistant* (1957; rept., Harmondsworth: Penguin, 1971), pp. 183, 112-13.

42. Walter Shear, "Culture Conflict," in Leslie A. and Joyce W. Field, eds., *Bernard Malamud and the Critics* (New York: New York UP, 1970), p. 208.

43. Malamud, p. 20; Ihab Hassan, "The Qualified Encounter," in Field, eds., *Malamud*, p. 200.

44. Though Malamud's later novels move away from the subject, he also explores

immigrant themes in a number of his short stories: see his collections entitled *Idiots First* (1963) and *The Magic Barrel* (1958), both reprinted (Harmondsworth: Penguin, 1966 and 1968).

45. Philip Roth, *Goodbye, Columbus and Five Short Stories* (1959; rept., London: Corgi, 1971), pp. 64, 6, 18.

46. Ibid. For the critics, see Jermey Larner, "The Conversion of the Jews," *Partisan Review*, **27** (1960), 761-68, and Irving Howe, "Philip Roth Reconsidered," *Commentary*, **54** (1972), 69-77.

47. Malcolm Bradbury, *The Expatriate Tradition in American Literature* (1982), the ninth pamphlet in this series.

Also of interest to readers of this pamphlet:

6. THE AMERICAN DREAM, by Robert H. Fossum and John K. Roth

What is "The American Dream"? So often casually used to denote American aspirations, the phrase eludes simple definition. For the Dream is and always has been comprised of many, sometimes conflicting visions. Reflecting on the writings of representative American figures from the colonial period to the present, this pamphlet reveals that although the visions have undergone various historical permutations, they also contain recurrent themes — especially that of new beginnings — which give the Dream a subtle unity. In the past few decades, even those elements have been called into question, however, leaving many Americans with ambivalent feelings at best, a sense of downright betrayal at worst, about a Dream that threatens to end in nightmare.

9. THE EXPATRIATE TRADITION IN AMERICAN LITERATURE, by Malcolm Bradbury

From the Revolution to the present day, many American writers have chosen to live in Europe — with considerable consequences for American art and consciousness. This pamphlet suggests such expatriation represented not so much a rejection of America as a response to deep-rooted cultural problems: it considers the difficulties of American writers in creating a national culture, and the many stages of their connection with European movements and art forms. Looking at major authors and texts — Irving, Cooper, Hawthorne, James, Stein, Eliot, Pound, Hemingway, Fitzgerald, Henry Miller — and their artistic and social context, it emphasizes the importance of a 'comparative' approach to American literature, and the persistence of artistic and intellectual attachments which have sustained the interconnections of contemporary Western culture.

Obtainable from the address on the inside back cover.

Other pamphlets now available:

Obtainable from address on the opposite page.